Motherland

MOTHERLAND

POEMS BY
Sally Thomas

ABLE MUSE PRESS

Able Muse Press

www.ablemusepress.com

Printed in the United States of America

Library of Congress Control Number: 2019937301

ISBN 978-1-77349-043-4 (paperback)
ISBN 978-1-77349-044-1 (digital)

Cover image: "Beyond the Fog" by Martin Sattler

Cover & book design by Alexander Pepple

Able Muse Press is an imprint of *Able Muse:* A Review of Poetry, Prose & Art—at www.ablemuse.com

Able Muse Press
467 Saratoga Avenue #602
San Jose, CA 95129

Acknowledgments

My grateful acknowledgments go to the editors of the following publications where these poems, some in earlier versions, first appeared:

Ascent: "White Morning, Crows"

Dappled Things: "For You," "Lamplight," and "Richeldis of Walsingham"

First Things: "Bees," "Exercise," "Foster Child," "Snow Weather," and "Sonnet for Ash Wednesday"

Modern Age: "Bridge Morning," "Dolphins," and "Tableau"

Mezzo Cammin: "Hindsight"

North Carolina Literary Review: "Daybreak" and "Magus at Twilight"

Presence: "Obscure Constellation in Winter"

Ruminate: "Deer Apples"

Seam: "At the Millpond"

The Greensboro Review: "Girl on Roller Skates"

The Lost Country: "Aunts," "Burial in Holy Week," "Detachment," "Moonlight Sestina," and "Souvenir in Trier"

The New Yorker: "Reunion"

The Orchards Poetry Journal: "My Father Drawing in an Upstairs Room"

The Rialto: "Frost," "In a Café," and "Offering"

Wild Goose Poetry Review: "In That Place," "Laundromat," and "Storm Season"

Willow Springs: "Grandmother Rising"

Windhover: "Angelus" and "Lookout Mountain"

Some of the poems in this collection have appeared in two chapbooks, *Fallen Water* (2015) and *Richeldis of Walsingham* (2016), both from Finishing Line Press. "Poem in Advent" first appeared in *Life and Times of LSM: A Living History*, published by the Vicar and Churchwardens of Saint Mary the Less, Cambridge, UK. I acknowledge with gratitude the generosity of the vicar and churchwardens in including the poem as part of the parish's historical record.

I am grateful to many mentors and friends, living and deceased, whose readings of individual poems and the manuscript as a whole, over the course of many years, helped to bring this book to fruition. These include Joseph Bottum, Sharon Bryan, Mark Jarman, Jacqueline Osherow, Anne Stevenson, and Mark Strand, as well as my classmates at the University of Memphis and the University of Utah. Also, I wish to thank the people who have lived with me through the writing of these poems, over many years: my husband, Ron, and my children, Ada, Joel, Ben, and Rachel. Everywhere I go, they are my motherland.

Foreword

SALLY THOMAS IS A POET who has looked out upon the world through the senses as with the intellect, in an intensity of engagement that is rare in the poetry of any age. Thomas first *sees* and then *embodies*, in precise language and the strict patterns of formal verse, her observations of people, places, weather, flora, and fauna, in a universe that has been called an "open mystery," yet which can also be understood, in Christian terms, as *the* Creation brought into being by God as the first and greatest Maker, and celebrated by Thomas as a "maker" (poet) herself, engaged in the craft (the "mystery") of verse. Thomas has, as once was said of C.S. Lewis, "a mind awake." What she sees and gives us are perceptions of a richer, fuller world.

The title of her collection—*Motherland*—captures, in a single word, this fuller world: Thomas's own motherhood; Mother Nature; the maternal birthing of poems; English as Thomas's mother tongue (she lived for some years in Cambridge, England, the Mother Country, where some poems are set); Mother Church (Thomas is a convert to Roman Catholicism); and Mary as the Mother of God, especially as Mary is seen in the remarkable sequence, Richeldis of Walsingham, which closes the book.

Like Wordsworth, or Hopkins, Thomas has the power to remove the scales of custom from our eyes so that we see the world anew—or perhaps better said, we see the world in something approaching its wholeness. The world she perceives is material but more than matter alone. It is also a world of spirit, myth, sacramental sign, and incarnation. As Blake wrote, "The Atoms of Democritus/ And Newton's Particles of Light/ Are sands upon the Red Sea shore/ Where Israel's tents do shine so bright." Or, as Thomas herself says, looking at the stars, deep in night, in the poem "Lamplight," "More light than theirs seemed hidden in that place."

Thomas's poems are, and are about, what may be called *literal symbols speaking for themselves*, the sign and the thing as one, an imitation of, and, ultimately, a participation in the Eucharist of the church and a Eucharist of creation. As the Roman Catholic Welsh poet David Jones deeply believed, to be human is to "act 'sacramentally'"; for it is the nature of man to be a maker of myths and signs that have been "extending frontiers the other side of time" and that reveal, as Jacques Maritain has called it, the radiance of the ontological mystery. Such poetry is a kind of thanksgiving.

In order to see and then embody in words this fuller, more radiant world, Thomas aspires to what the great English poet Geoffrey Hill once called a poem: "an act of total attention." Such attention must be wholly realized in the words of the poem, and, like many other poets, Thomas knows the power, ambiguity, shared ownership, and limits of language. As she says, "We think in a language/ At once ours and not ours" ("New Year's Day")—as with a word spoken in a wedding vow: ". . . *cleave*,/ That strange word that means/ Its opposite." Therefore the poet must hone language to her purpose. As she says of the birds in "White Morning, Crows," "They speak a language/ Distilled to one syllable,// Seamless and sharp/ As what I want to say."

What Thomas wants to say is both embedded in, and yet also filtered through, many subjects keenly observed: her life as wife and mother, a minor constellation, birds (falcon, starling, crow), deer apples, the habits of bees, her garden like Eden in its fallen state, the church's liturgical calendar, the sounds and rhythms of a baby nursing blending with changes rung on church bells nearby—and many more.

Lines from "Poem in Advent" illustrate Thomas's method at its best. The poem begins with a picture. (Thomas's titles often seem like the titles of paintings though her poems are not static word pictures but full of action.)

> At twilight the poplars, upright and naked,
> Wear starlings like restless leaves. Unafflicted
>
> By the cold, they come and go in noisy shifts,
> Filling the trees, free-falling into updrafts
>
> Which lift them—corporate, voluntary smoke-rings—
> To surf the air above the roofs.

By the poem's end, this seemingly purely natural depiction becomes something *enhanced* by the poet's observation that the bare trees—backlit by a fiery twilight—hold the birds in darkness in a way that is subtly suggestive of something beyond mere description:

> The clamorous starling
> Host rises, falls, a black swirling
>
> On the sky. As one winged mind, it comes to roost
> Where there's no shelter, only wet branches tossed
>
> Like skeleton flames, ignited by the wind.
> Darkness, careful, cups them in its hand.

Read carefully, these lines—without in any way disturbing or distorting the accuracy of the mere observation of starlings, twilight, dark, and trees—bring together the natural order and the Christian understanding of Advent and the Incarnation with a divinely encompassing protectiveness and love. Behind Thomas's lines we all but hear those prophetic words spoken during Advent: "The people that have walked in darkness have seen a great light" (Isaiah 9:2).

Near the end of the first of the two major sections of *Motherland* is a poem entitled "Bees." Like the starlings of "Poem in Advent," the bees are on a journey through the world. And like the minor constellation the Giraffe or like seagulls—of which Thomas writes in other poems—the bees lack any conscious knowledge of purpose or intention or final end. Yet these creatures, in their own way, are as the poet is—going through life on her own "pilgrimage of habit" not only as a thinker, *Homo sapiens*, but also as *Homo faber* ("man the maker"), in her case, the maker as poet practicing the habits of the craft.

The second half of *Motherland* balances the first half in also being about a pilgrimage and motherhood, this time, that of Mary the Mother of Christ and the story of the famous shrine to Mary at Walsingham, England.[1]

---

1   My comments on the poems in the sequence *Richeldis of Walsingham* are adapted from my review of Thomas's chapbook by the same title. This review was originally published in *Dappled Things: A Quarterly of Ideas, Art, and Faith*, Candlemas 2018, 13.1, 109–114.

Richeldis of Walsingham was a Saxon noblewoman who, in 1061, had visions of the Virgin Mary in which Richeldis was transported to the Holy Family's house in Nazareth. Mary told Richeldis to build a replica of this house in Walsingham as a shrine for veneration by pilgrims. And so, over the next almost five hundred years, the Shrine of Our Lady of Walsingham—with its holy well and spring—came to be, after Canterbury with its Shrine of St. Thomas Becket, the second most popular destination in England for pilgrims. It became known as "England's Nazareth."

At the Slipper Chapel, these pilgrims—including even a younger Henry VIII—removed their shoes to walk the final "Holy Mile" to the Marian shrine. In 1538, during the time of the dissolution of the monasteries, the shrine at Walsingham, along with nearby monastic orders and their buildings, was suppressed and destroyed. Its statue of Mary was taken away to London where, in September of 1538, it was publicly burned. But the shrine could not be obliterated from the memory of the people, and, in the late nineteenth and the twentieth century, both an Anglican and a Roman Catholic shrine were built in Walsingham, which city now receives thousands of pilgrims every year.

Thomas's poems about Richeldis, the shrine, Walsingham, the natural beauty of Norfolk, and other people associated with the shrine range widely over time. Three that share the same title *richeldis circa 1080*— are about the shrine's founder. The other poems have double titles—the same word, but given first in Anglo-Saxon and then in modern English. This journeying through time and through the history of the language is thus interwoven with the history of the shrine: its founding in 1061, its destruction in 1538, its rebuilding in the twentieth century, and its eternal significance as a doorway between this world and the world beyond.

The spirit of the late Middle Ages is beautifully captured in what is perhaps this section's finest poem: "*wife (woman) 1323*." Spoken by a lady who married her lord when he was thirty and she was just fourteen, the poem begins with the marriage ceremony:

> Thirty to my fourteen: my wedded lord.
> The church so cold our white breaths colored

The air, small clouds
The shape of words
I scarcely remembered afterwards.

But soon her husband falls sick of some contagious disease, and the young wife stays by his side, day and night, until he dies: "His hand cooled in mine." Now, she visits his resting-place inside the church:

Each morning at Mass
My shadow falls across
His staring face

Graven into the floor. Once
I went back alone and knelt to kiss
The polished slab that keeps his bones in place.

Taken as a whole, Thomas's Richeldis poems are a fascinating history of the Shrine of Our Lady of Walsingham. There is no single narrative line followed chronologically. Rather, the poems are lyrical meditations that combine precise imagery of everyday human experiences and of natural beauty with elusive yet fascinating states of soul, mind, and feeling. And the skillful use of enjambment, full rhymes, and partial rhymes adds a kind of resonant quietude to this world of the commonplace and the mystical. The Richeldis poems succeed admirably in creating memorable and evocative scenes from the long history of the shrine—including pilgrims, the people of Walsingham, the shrine itself, and the natural beauty of Norfolk that are associated with it.

THE POEMS OF SALLY THOMAS are poems in which the act of *looking* at the world in all its depth and complexity is just about as close as possible to being fully realized in the corresponding "world" of poetic language and form. And the verses are compelling because in every line something is *at stake*: our very understanding of creation, the human condition, and the mystery of thought and its language that link us, however imperfectly, to what may be called the *given* world. As Thomas says in "Frost," "Tricky winter light and my own eye/ Bend the world, if not to beauty, then/ To strangeness."

In the end, the world that Thomas so deeply apprehends is—for the human observer—a place of danger, wonder, beauty, evil, good, relationship, isolation, anxiety, passion, pain, and adventure. Yet this world seems to exist in and of itself, unaware, and thus indifferent to the human need to know and interpret and give a meaning to things, perhaps even to disclose a meaning somehow already embedded *in* things.

This is the riven ground that the poet as wordsmith, sign maker, and builder of metaphorical-symbolic bridges is called upon to cross. In so doing, the poet comes closer to seeing things in their fullness of being, as in Thomas's poem "Lookout Mountain": "When all the earth is wheeling with the stars/ Through darkness. . . / . . . Creation begs the driving-all-night mind/ Behind the wheel, *Look out—Look out—Look out—*." To *look out*: to beware, to be *a*-ware, and to look outside the window of the self at the world—this is our privilege as human beings as we journey through time, going along upon the pilgrim way to the end of our own lives, to Walsingham—a shrine restored—and then at last to a greater restoration yet to be.

David Middleton
Poet in Residence Emeritus
Nicholls State University
Thibodaux, Louisiana
February 2019

Contents

xvi

Motherland

Change-Ringing

You remember church bells, mainly,
A wordless shape-note singing
On the sky. Nightly, daily,
As the baby fed, their ringing

Echoed the rhythm of sigh
And suck, the lashes fluttering
On the flushed cheek. You try
To sort through images cluttering

Your mind's dark attic, and
That's what you come up with: bells.
Not your baby's fisted hand,
His warm and varied smells,

His wandering slate-blue gaze,
The dampness of his hair.
What you find are clanging days
And midnights in some chair,

Half-dreaming, while that clamor
Wavered the windowpane.
Caught by the memory's glamor,
You nod in your chair again,

And nurse this living weight
Your heart's received. What of it?
Recalling bells in the twilight,
Distractedly you love it.

In That Place

Sometimes from the window you'd see a woman pass
In the street below, bent to the task of pushing

Her baby's pram heavy with daily shopping.
You'd see her plod through rain, her thoughts opaque

To you as the sky that veiled the wet white sun.
You too had a pram, and children. You walked beneath windows.

You pushed your little loneliness up the road.
In those distant days, your days were made of footsteps,

To school, to market, across Midsummer Common,
Along the towpath, where narrowboats rode their moorings.

Remember that boat you loved for her name alone:
Unthinkable. There, again, you've thought of her.

You walked into town, past shops selling halal meats,
Buckets of brussels sprouts knobbled and alien,

Their stalks looking ready to burst into glorious bloom,
If you didn't know better. See, this too you remember.

You must have existed. There were your children. Always
You stopped at the bakery first to buy them sausage rolls.

One baby cried. Another uncurled inside you,
Thumping her hidden fists on the taut, slick walls.

Everywhere you went, you were her motherland.
Night fell. In the rain, headlights ran downstream.

Looking up, you'd see the lamps left on
In a window—yours—exhaling gold in the dark.

Home was a thing you made out of light and warmth.
Life is a thing you make of what you've discovered

Behind you: rain, children, yes, and loneliness,
That lullaby you find yourself humming now

As you lean your forehead against the cold dark window
And see, in the street, a young woman walking by

Pushing a baby. What does she hope will happen?
She turns the corner. None of us can stay.

Obscure Constellation in Winter

Bare trees snag the sunset now. No birds
Gather in the slanted light to call
The evening in. Graying, bald, it girds

Itself against itself. At this hour, all
The little varied fires you tried to start
Sink to embers. Dirty dishes oversprawl

Your kitchen. The whole house threatens to outsmart
You again. Today, on rising, you made coffee.
You made the bed. You meant to make an art

Of work. A gift. Felt nothing. Didn't see
Your purpose there. *The stars cannot love God*—
Or so you've read—*because they are not free.*

I don't love God, I think you might have said
As you swept clean, again, again, your floors:
Dust-drifts, cobwebs, a single crisply dead

Cockroach. Out, out. At least you took no prisoners,
You say. Tonight, the Giraffe's begun to shine
In his faint, frosted uphill winter course.

He perseveres. Of course he'll never win,
Or lose, either. He'll simply go on being
Almost invisible, but there. By some volition

Not his own, he'll run. He's neither fleeing
Any enemy, nor pressing to any goal.
It's not himself he pleases. Deaf, unseeing,

He glitters in the heavens' upturned bowl.
As you step, tearful, into the bracing air,
Shut the door behind you. Reclaim your soul.

Decide to. From your back step, find him there.
Perhaps something will come to you, some words
That as you think them almost could be prayer.

Angelus

Be it done, you say, a noonday habit.
Unconceived, your children wait for you.
Neat rows of them hang quiet in the mind's
Upstairs closet. Like dresses never worn,

Your unconceived children have been waiting.
You told them that of course you'd wear them all
Someday. The upstairs closet's long locked,
A room outside your life. Now you stand praying

As you might stand there wondering what to wear.
Somehow it's never this dress, never that one.
With room now in your life, you stand praying.
One of them could choose you by surprise.

Would it be this dress? That dress? Somehow you
Don't care. They're timeless, never out of style.
One of them could choose you. The surprise
Would become you, as now sky-blue becomes you,

Carefree, timeless, never out of style.
Be it done to me, you say, *according*—
The words become you, though you're feeling blue,
Praying at your desk like this. Today

One thing may be done, and not the other.
Does this mean hope, or does it mean despair?
You're praying at your desk, and it's today,
When anything might happen. But those dresses,

Dark, unworn, locked upstairs in your mind,
Mock your nakedness. Hope feels like despair.
Still, anything can happen, any day
You wear your noonday habit. What's done is done.

Hindsight

Silence fell at daybreak, when an early
Riser or a late-to-bedder might
Glance out into nothingness, pierced only
By a bicycle's flickering red taillight

Dwindling into gray, a seagoing boat
That breasts the morning tide and, traveling down
The world's hazy curve, is lost to sight.
My memory likewise sets out from the known

World of things I'm sure I saw and heard,
Into murky unmapped waters. If I wrote,
Those were happier days, at which false word
Would the anchor drag? Or the opposite—

I cried buying clementines in the market—
If I say it, I cannot make it true,
Or truer than it is. *Coins in my pocket?*
Yes. Were they enough? That, I don't know.

I see now, in my mind, the clear pondwater
Aspect of a gusty winter sunset.
Starlings swirl like sediment. My daughter
Says—what?—as I watch them. I forget.

I remember how things looked, our narrow flat,
The lane rain-silvered. I can almost hear
Wind shivering through our windows. More than that?
It isn't there. It isn't anywhere.

New Year's Day

Cambridge, 2001

Seagulls surf the wet
Updrafts over roofs
    A hundred miles inland—

Every weather's a weather
        Of gulls, a scream against
The bottle-blue or cloud-mottled

        Sky, the one
Constant besides rain
        Spittling the window:

These birds who revel in being
        Blown off-course. If
They had any idea, that is,

        Where they meant
To go in the first place.

*

        I was never a believer

In resolutions. What's *resolve*
        But another word for *wish*?
Ask the fisherman's wife

How far she got on wishes.
Would I *resolve*, say, to let
　　A third child choose

Itself? What can I
　　Say I wish for? Just now
My two already-wished-for

　　Children, resolved into flesh,
Gallop down the hall,
　　Speaking in whinnies.

　　When I wrench the door open
And shout, *Inside feet!*
　　They look at me. What

Are *inside feet*? We have
　　The same feet wherever
We go. *Okay,*

　　They say. They wait
For the door to close. Gallop
　　Gallop, neigh neigh. Does control

End at conception? Or
　　Only our belief in it?

*

The rain's tsunami threatens

      To wash the whole country
Into its inhospitable
      Hinterland, the sea.

We inhabit a culture of rain,
      Learn to speak its commonplaces:
Wellieboots, waterproofs—as if

      We needed to prove water's
Existence. We think in a language
      At once ours and not ours.

At breakfast our son holds up
      A spoon. *What's the English
Word for this?* He won't believe

      That *spoon* could possibly be the answer.

*

Where does it come from, this desire
      To shape-shift, to be, say,

A horse for the afternoon?
      Perhaps some memory
Persists, of pre-life,

Or not *pre-life*, but life
Before it's named, flesh and blood,
        Yes, and also possibility.

Perhaps children remember
        Without knowing
That call that makes them

        Step so fluidly out
Of the familiar world, though
        Of course they don't

Leave it. The body
        Goes with them
Through the locked gates

        Into snowy pastures
Unprinted by any hooves.

*

        Empty branches tap

The leaded chapel window:
        Stainless daylight, white
Walls, the unprompted

        Revelation of the world
Not watching us at prayer—
        At the motions of prayer, our lips

Moving over words
        Which like our own names
Begin to lose sense

        When we overhear ourselves
Whispering them—not watching
        But with us, cold,

Immaculate, clear.

*

        Somehow we never imagined
Having to say, *Take your feet*

        Off the celery. Don't lick me.
The corkscrew is not a toy.
        What did we expect?

Amnesia, entropy
        Extend their present-tense
Mercies to our children who are

        Not whatever we dreamed,
Vague, two-dimensional
        Composites of our childhood

Photographs. Quiet. Able
        To play the piano. Sew.
Finish what they begin.

        Absolve us of ourselves.

*

After church, a friend
    Offers her baby, drinks

Her black coffee, grateful
    For a minute, two hands free.
The baby snuffles, exhales

    Warmly into my neck,
And I think, *Oh,*
    It didn't hurt so much.

And other lies, as if I thought
    Nothing of having hands
Open to take the weight

    Of a child who won't wake me
From an hour's sleep. This
    Can pass for a decision.

My translation of a word
    Like *goal.* Or *sane.*
I could fit a travel cot

    Between my bed and desk—
Anything's possible. Or if
    Impossible, still possibly worth doing.

*

Cot: what the baby
      Sleeps in. *Crib*: what
The manger becomes when surrounded

      By plaster statuettes wearing painted
Expressions of reverence or weariness—
      Never surprise, though you'd think

Somebody might have been surprised.

*

      In bed, in the borrowed
Time before the alarm,

      We hold each other, hoping
Maybe this time it won't
      Happen, the day will hang

Back shyly at its own
      Threshold. Even now
The sky is paling, a white

      Sliver between the curtains.
Eleven years married, are we
      Any closer to knowing

What we want? Our wedding
      Vows told us precious
Little. Not what to

Expect, only to *cleave*,
That strange word that means
　　　　Its opposite. I close

My eyes. This could be
　　　　A stranger's body my hands
Move across, mapping again

　　　　Desire's universal, alien terrain.

*

O for the wings—but where
　　　　Would I go? Where are you not?

All of you, husband, children,
　　　　Calling my name, calling me
Back from myself, back into

　　　　Myself. Erasable
Only by death. This
　　　　Must be what it means,

One flesh. I carry
　　　　Your voices in the pocket
Of my ear. We speak

　　　　Of *making* vows, love*making*,
As if such things didn't exist
　　　　Until we think.

And they occur to us.

*

Morning wind hurls itself
Against the house, forces rain
         In through the absence

Of caulking. In watery daylight
         Beached raindrops glint
Like jellyfish along

         The windowsill. Outside,
Birds are still free-falling
         Like leaves across the housetops,

         Blown away but
Never out of the sky.

Foster Child

Everywhere she goes he goes.
She's brought him here to Sunday tea.
He's been with me two weeks, she says,
And shifts him deftly on her knee.
The rest of us try not to see
The fine blue feed-tube in his nose
Or how his spine won't hold him up.
She says, *I've called him Samuel.*
He didn't have a name at all,
Just 'Baby Boy.' She sets her cup
Out of reach by habit. He
Eyes it warily. Gray dusk
Falls over everything: our grate
Laid for a fire, the book-stacked desk,
The clock, the cold remains of tea
The strainer holds. She says, *It's late.*
Please could I lay him down somewhere?
That's fine. He's not particular.

Settled in our travel cot,
He stares at her with old brown eyes,
Anxious, though, *He never cries,*
She boasts. *Good boy. We'll see if he's*
Adoptable. What if he's not?
The thing is, you can never keep
A child. They go their way. We snap
The light off, leave the door ajar.
In the other room, before the fire,

All settled now, we sit and drink.
The sherry and the evening sink.
Firelight shudders on the floor,
In the darkening window where
Our reflected faces loom and pass
Like faces glancing from a bus,
Watching us briefly, and through these
Apparitions, the empty trees.

For You

Am I your favorite? you want to know,
So I say yes: As every breath I take's
My favorite breath. If, say, you're eight, that makes
You my favorite eight-year-old. Ditto
Seven, six, five, four, three, two, one, zero.
You were my favorite series of summer earthquakes,
My favorite live-weight centered on the cervix,
My favorite sight unseen that year. And so
You are my favorite child right now, because
You stand before me, asking that my heart
Declare, *You first, you always*. And it's true.
It works this way. Love's strange, elastic laws
Grant each child its undiluted part,
And that, my love, is what I offer you.

Bridge Morning

The child outside the swinging door
Heard her mother say,
I won't make something of myself
Stuck at home all day.

Honey, said a languid voice,
Some days I'm so depressed
By toilet bowls and groceries
I almost can't get dressed.

Another friend remarked, *I told*
My husband that. I said,
'Lanier, you hear me out. I am
Too young to feel this dead.'

I saw my doctor, cried a third.
He said to me, 'Miz Wade,
You get a little job and leave
That child home with the maid.'

All the while, the pattering cards
Were shuffled, dealt, and drawn.
Ice rattled in the glasses. Outside,
S.E. mowed the lawn.

The child sat on her leather stool
Behind the swinging door
And watched Princetta move across
The chessboard of the floor.

Princetta's hands were black and broad,
Their palms pale-pink as lips
Before the public smile's drawn on
In red. Around her hips

White apron strings, crisscrossed and tied,
Strained as she bent to see
Light biscuits rising, and to sieve
Black silted leaves from tea.

Child, Princetta said, *you scoot.*
You in Princetta's way.
She backed out through the swinging door
With her heavy silver tray.

Girl on Roller Skates

She sat on the boardinghouse steps
Scratching chigger bites. That year,
She was eight years old, barelegged,
Sweaty from skating the length
Of the block to the movie theater
And back. Beside her, her grandmother
Drank watery tea, smoked Luckies,
Her flowered dress wet in half-circles
Though she held her arms out for the air,
Sweat-wet itself, to circulate.
She dispensed advice to the girl,
Who deserved it. Without any wind,
The collards in the garden swished,
Saying, *Ladies wear hats, darling. And gloves.*

Inside, the girl's older sister played
Piano for the lady boarders nodding
Over greasy canasta cards.
The little sister fiddled with her skate key,
Glad to be banished outside,
Away from the decorous whine
Of the fan wired into the window,
The rooms' green high-ceilinged gloom.
Honey, nobody wants to marry
A girl with scabs on her knees.
She did not want to be a lady.
She did not want to marry anyone.
Just then, her own face was enough,

Emerging from the hallway darkness,
White and unsurprised in the mirror,
Pursing its lips for a kiss.

Nobody likes a vain girl.
But how was it vain, she wondered,
To want to know what you look like?
All day long she had to remind herself,
Just as she might practice seeing
The rows of soldiers jittering
Past the Movietone cameras, practice
Saying to herself, *There's a war on.*
Things almost made sense, then: living
There, in that house, that town.
Her mother on the Memphis train.
Her father's letters saved in the Bible.
The spinster boarders' girdles and brassieres
Dripping above the bathtub, dead
Flies peppering windowsills, heat
Pressing her down at night
So she couldn't sleep, all meant
Something, even if it was
That there was nothing else after all.
She locked one skate across her toes.
The shadows exhaled their black breath.
She stood up steady on her skates.
When she moved, the wet air stood aside.

Lookout Mountain

A prayer for my son

At midnight I imagine you awake,
Shade rolled up, your window full of stars
Except where those black shoulders blot them out.
Big as a house, if houses were like mountains,
It hunkers on the sky. And you, awake,
May see it now, and marvel that it sleeps
When all the earth is wheeling with the stars
Through darkness. May you no longer mind
The thought that even these rock-rooted mountains
White-knuckle it, that even while it sleeps
Creation begs the driving-all-night mind
Behind the wheel, *Look out—Look out—Look out—*

Deer Apples

While you're still wondering what happened to the spring,
In cool moonlight and the crickets' whispering,

The season turns. No more bridal lace.
Purplish heat flushes the shifting face

Roadside dogwoods wear, this hurried day.
Back home, you're chopping apples to put away

In the deep-freeze for the winter: soft, bruised windfalls—
Deer apples, people say—the fruit stand sells

Six dollars for a twenty-odd-pound box,
To bait hunters' stands. Worm-bitten Gala, Cox,

Granny Smith, some little ones whose name
You don't know, all together breathe the same

Ripe smell, almost fermented. Now you cut
The grainy flesh right down to the chambered heart,

Rigid as cartilage, where the black seeds nest.
You fill ten Ziploc bags, but mound the best,

Least-bitten apples in a bowl. It used to be
That passing children ate them up immediately.

Who'll eat them now, before they liquefy
Inside their loosening skins? *A waste*, you'd cry,

Except that in this moment they're a feast
To look at, heaped together in the last

Off-kilter light—curvaceous, red, or gold
As pollen, wax-cheeked, radiantly cold.

Snow Weather

A falcon on a wire
Against the laden sky
Scanned his brown empire
With a black-ice eye.

Nothing beneath him stirred
In that sunless instant,
But my heart, for a keen-eyed bird
Blind to me, or indifferent.

Poem in Advent

At twilight the poplars, upright and naked,
Wear starlings like restless leaves. Unafflicted

By the cold, they come and go in noisy shifts,
Filling the trees, free-falling into updrafts

Which lift them—corporate, voluntary smoke-rings—
To surf the air above the roofs. Smudge of wings,

Harbinger of every winter nightfall,
The robin's opposite, they're never mournful.

The day's withdrawal isn't an antithesis
To hope. Let the evening draw its noose

Tighter. Let tires on the wet pavement
Sigh, *From night you came. Where else but night*

Do you belong? Should you despair? The clamorous starling
Host rises, falls, a black swirling

On the sky. As one winged mind, it comes to roost
Where there's no shelter, only wet branches tossed

Like skeleton flames, ignited by the wind.
Darkness, careful, cups them in its hand.

Christmas Day in the Morning

My lady takes the pins from her hair,
Lets the heavy plaits fall. The sweaty nurse,
Half-asleep in the corner, hides her face
From a white streak of sunlight on the floor.

As it should, the day breaks clear
And hard. The basin-water's turned to ice.
In the courtyard, a clamor of geese,
Dogs quarreling underfoot, and everywhere

The blind cold, the dumbstruck wind.
In the crib, the staring child. My lady goes
On working the hard comb through her undone hair.

Bells crack apart the brittle air,
Shake the walls, shake the saints, their flat haloes,
The painted Christ, cold lilies in His hand.

Magus at Twilight

If we retraced our steps, what would we find?
Street names changed, nothing we'd recognize.
Strange faces, or none, at staring windows.
Not that we knew anyone. Every man
Pushing past in the crowd was a stranger
Like us. Only we didn't sign our name.

On the other hand, we might find the town
Restored to itself: doddering, asleep
Beneath ordinary winter starlight.
Nothing happening, no call for an inn
Except as a lamplit place where old men
Drink another silent round together.

Recall, all dark outbuildings look the same.
We'd never know which it was, or whether
The one we wanted hadn't been torn down.
Imagine us three going door to door,
Telling some incredulous householder,
Cows. A donkey, maybe. Also some sheep—
As if he'd smack his head and say, *Oh, THAT.*

Put the dream away. Of what we saw there,
Nothing's left, surely. Pass me the last wine
And the heel of that bread. It's cold tonight.
Look, a light's come shivering down the lane.
Only an oil lamp—joiner's boy home late.
His small flame sputters in the rising wind.

Frost

Sun-struck at noon, the stiffened grass
Stands blades-up, hilts-down, like buried knives
That from this window-distance simply glitter:
Fool's gold, fool's silver, fool's snow.

On the roped-off cricket pitches, seagulls natter,
Their scrappy whiteness dark against the whiteness
Of frost and full-bore sunshine. Every shadow
Shrinks into what casts it. Nothing moves

Or seems to move, though three teenaged boys
Knock a football back and forth—is it lunch break
Already?—watched by blue-sweatshirted girls
Who elbow, laugh, and pass around a smoke.

The fag-end brightens on their lips. Their small noise
Splinters on the brittle air; it whirls
Up in white wingbeats and dissolves
With a shriek into the sky—

Tricky winter light and my own eye
Bend the world, if not to beauty, then
To strangeness, on which the cold sun
Shines, and the grass shines back like knives.

Tableau

Cold daylight fills the nave
As water in a glass
Stands upright, a clear cylinder.
Three women, come for Mass

At lunchtime on a weekday
When it's Father and themselves,
Confer in hisses at the door—
Sacristy something shelves

Want cleaning. In the churchyard,
Beneath a leafless tree,
A woman smokes, swaddled in coats,
And stares broodingly

Through the gray viney tangle
To the lane beyond the fence.
A man steps off his bicycle,
Chains it, then repents.

Muttering, he unlocks it
And cycles off again.
The smoker watches his retreat.
The other three have gone

Into the church, still whispering,
While the tower bell says *clong*.
The smoker casts her fag-end down
And moves herself along.

Daybreak

The trees shrug off the faded dark as you'd
Flick rusty tapwater from your fingers in
Some gas-station john so filthy you avoid
Touching the paper towels. Across town,
On a wedge of land between two highways' knees,
A rented double-wide's burned to its metal bones.
Nothing to see but a glum woman eating Cheez-
Its. In the pallid light of her salvaged cell phone's
Screen she thumbs some message. *Wear r u?*
What's the answer? Where, now, is he or she,
Husband, lover, mama? What's gone wrong?
She lights a cigarette, breathes bitter blue.
Hidden in the one shining dogwood tree,
A mockingbird unravels a stray end of song.

Morning, with Goldfinches

Last March, too, these pairs came
To our feeders in marital
Exaltations. Quarrel
And rapture played daily on our
Drawn drapes, a theater
Of flitting shadows. Mornings, when
We twitched back one curtain,
The struck air reverberated.
The winged resonance fled.
Males were all in patchy gray molt.
Gold bled through at each throat.
Scattering thistle seed, sparring,
They ate while, marveling
In each other's arms, we watched them.

In each other's arms, we watched them
Light and leave, brief as light.
All living things have the same bright
Fleetness, though we don't see—
We aren't struck by it the same way,
All the time. It hides deep
In some creatures: in us, who sleep
Even when we wake, who
Lie abed late and wonder too
Little at shadows that
Play on the white wall opposite.
Too soon, they're washed away
In darkness. So goes every day,
Granted its human name.

Granted its human name,
This day enters. All days answer
To their names, given to honor
Fixed and permanent things:
Gods, sun, moon, immortal shinings
In changeless skies. Except
Skies do change. In the high transept
Window, clouds gallop, then
Lay their tumbled white garments down.
We sleep, we rise, we die
Again briefly in sleep. The sky
Holds our mirror. We see
Our lives in it, swift as a day
Full of wings, trees in flame.

Full of wings, trees in flame
Like angels, all white light, the spring
Comes. A sweet beginning
Wreathed in bluebells, with sharp weather.
Long mornings, together,
We'll soon hear goldfinches' flinty
Calls in the cold. Plenty
Of thistle seed. Still they'll fight. We'll
Smile to recall their shrill
Back-and-forth, their scrappy angers,
Small lordships. Their hunger's
In all things, new, sunlit, nesting—
In us, too, then, resting
In our familiar selves, at home.

In our familiar selves, at home
In flesh we wear each day,
The strangeness lies. You are the way
I live—and what is that?
Parryings. Laughter. All the bright
Daily passings-away
The world's made of. Sweet brevity,
Newest hour, everything
Most lovely, most loved, goes singing.
Shadows wing across light.
Curtains drawn still against the night,
Let's lie here, you and I,
Be stirred one more fresh season by
Brief hungers, and succumb.

Sonnet for Ash Wednesday

On a tomb in Little Saint Mary's Church, Cambridge

Here lyeth . . . (Sarah?) Drake beneath the floor,
A Persian carpet lapped across her stone,
So all you see is—*rah* and *Cambridgeshire*
And that she was the cherished wife of someone
Who caused her to sleep before the altar
Like Samuel, consigned to night and God.
Mutely, being dead, she bears the thurifer
Who stands on her, swinging his silver pod
Of incense like a pendulum. What time
Is it, six feet down? How long did they
Tell her the wait would be? And is her name
Written where it matters, legibly,
Or will we all, given the same name—*Dust*—
Forget at last who was forgotten first?

Burial in Holy Week

All our lives are just an eyelash, said my friend
Beside her baby's grave. The troubled sky
Galloped above the narrow cold red wound
Opened in violet-starred grass. A monastery
Graveyard: a strange, apt place for a girl to find
Herself in white, an involuntary bride
In a celibate communion, facing God
Who had given and received in one dread day.
The little box was settled into earth,
Heavy coverlet turned up, the clotted clay
Spaded smooth. Then, having seen this birth
Complete, the new womb closed, the other children
Ran laughing among the modest, ordered headstones
In the wind, beneath the veiled and sinking sun—
Alive as fire, brief and hungry, with that abandon
Which is a kind of praise—throwing pinecones.

Holy Saturday

On reading an ancient homily for the day

Something strange is happening today,
A mundane Saturday of sun and wind.
Awake, O sleeper, Christ has gone to say—

To whom? This year my father's led astray
In death. For him and others, struck clay-blind,
What strange thing is happening today?

Beneath the damp moss where tree-shadows play
In chancy sun, does Christ extend His hand
To these new dead? Beckoning, does He say,

They've missed you? This last Christmas made them cry?
Time's moved on. When will we see it end?
Something strange is happening today,

But not for them or us, not yet. If we
Tell them, *Sleep well*, we don't mean it's pretend.
Awake, O sleeper, we say Christ will say,

In the earth and under it. Lord, I hope they
Hear, who rest this morning, earth-stopped, root-bound.
Sleepers, wake. Christ comes to you to say,
Something strange is happening today.

Exercise

In certain lights our garden looked almost—
Not habitable, exactly, but like a garden:
Sudden daffodils, an unexpected host
Of primrose like grounded moths. Imagine Eden
In the aftermath, boxwoods outgrowing
Their bequeathed rounded, cornered, or conical
Shapes. Dropped limbs. Grass needing mowing.
Windfalls liquefied, an alcoholic smell,
Last summer's hindsight. Fruit flies
Ascending like visible, audible breath.
Imagine, against the wall, a rusted cooker
Showered with damp white blooms. Imagine an onlooker
At an open window, saying, *Ah, here's death
Undone again*, and glad of the exercise.

At the Millpond

Punts knock together. Chains slide
Back on the teak hulls. White chain-mail
Swims the stone bridge's underside,
A visual echo. Exciting? *Dull dull dull,*
These girls say, circled round their teacher
On the grass here, where the Cam backwashes, spills
Itself, light-fractured, into greener
Deeps below the race. Now the mill's
A pasta restaurant where you can sit
Watching, through a window in the floor,
The dark water's suck and slop. But is it
Interesting? What's happening? What's to see?
Pubs, the girls say. *And there's a dog.*
Miss Smith's group are getting ice cream. A tall lady
Stands above the weir with bread in a bag,
Coaxing cygnets. *Du kleine,* she calls each one.
Is this interesting? Or are we merely here?
The water breaks, resettles in the sun.

Epithalamion for a Renewal of Vows

After rain, all the fallen water's
Seeped away. But here, where this flat-top
Rock, weather-hollowed, holds back
The slope of the garden from the drive,
Stands a pool, a little eye gazing up
At what gave it to the ground.

In the morning, it shines there. By noon
The sun will have licked it dry.
It won't squirm with larvae like the birdbath.
No fresh-winged life will climb from it
To join forces with the air.
It's a brevity—

Still, there it is. You're seeing it
Because you looked down, because
You were outside this early, rain
Over and gone, whistling answers to the wren
Who asks the day where his love is.

Your love's in the kitchen making coffee.
And although you may never think
To mention this wet eye in its shallow
Cistern—because, let's face it,
Rain falls on rocks every day—

You might pour water on it now
And again, make it brim, an unspoken
Endearment that won't spill over,
So that maybe in the afternoon some bird
Will light there and drink.

Anniversary

All those years ago we stood in our good clothes
Before everyone we knew, and also God,
Who knowing us saw how the vows we made
Would endure us, though they cracked and warped with use.
Still, they serve. Every day we choose
Not to unsay them, as we don't leave our bed
A surf of twisted sheets, striped mattress naked
To the morning's merciless white gaze.

I'm tucking in the corners while you pin
Your black socks together for the wash.
They won't be separated. It's a small
Thing. Still, this morning I'm so grateful
You've pinned your socks together for the wash,
I'd dress up now and marry you again.

Souvenir in Trier

Green oil smoked and caught. One murky light
Went bobbing one time through one finite night

Here on the northern edge of an ordered world
Shrinking inside its borders. The oil-smoke curled

Invisibly on the darkness and was gone.
The lamp survived to nest, a squat clay hen,

On the shop lady's palm. *Sehr gut?* she said,
Feigning patience. Fifty deutschmarks for a dead

Zippo, or its enduring antiquarian
Equivalent, dug up from some Valerian-

Era street-beneath-a-street, common as dirt
Itself—was it worth that? Would a t-shirt

Have meant more, or a postcard matted and framed
To say, *We were here*? A lamp that flamed

Once, briefly, and was thrown away:
Does it revive for us that chancy day

Of sun, rain, each other, in that town
At the end of the straight road, where the stone

Walls rose, fell, were scattered, all but one
Time-black segment standing in unveiled sun

To be photographed and photographed by us
And forty Japanese, whose crimson bus

Snorted as it waited in the street?
Blink went forty-one shutters. That was it.

A woman wiped her lens, and then her sunglasses
With special tissue. So each moment passes

Into darkness and is lost. What passed between
The Black Gate and the shop remains unseen.

Did we eat ice cream? Did you hold my hand?
Was I morning-sick? *Mein freund, mein freund,*

I can't remember. Only the shop-room, dim
After the brilliant street. Only the lady's firm

Question: *So?* Her impassive silhouette.
What else did she have to sell us? I forget.

In a Café

You aren't supposed to see him hold her hand
Under the table, or hear how they speak
Their tragic dialect, always whispered,
Without resolution. Who won't be hurt?
You aren't supposed to see her weep her children
Into the unfurled dove-wing of her napkin.

There are no safe landings. No one's asking you
To imagine their lovemaking—they themselves
May only dream the unbuttoning, the tasting,
The gazing or not-gazing upon the body,
More naked than naked once fidelity's
Final intimate layer has fallen away.

Still, imagining is doing. Stripped, murmuring,
They conspire at their corner table. The smoky light
Catches the random silver in her hair
—You're not supposed to know any of this—
Trying to make her—just once—look up.

Introvert

He loves her inwardness, the private glance
Like a sunrise from her heart, a measured shine.
Still, after twenty years with her he wants
To prise her open, bone from hinging bone—
As needed—to expose the secret soul.
She keeps it close. But does she keep it for him?
Once his deliberate touch has made her whole,
He tells himself today, she'll start to blossom,
A forced narcissus like the ones his mother
Used to have at Christmas. In the sunlit
Living-room window they bloomed each year, another
Certain, seasonless spring. New flowers set
By old fronds' dying back, they stood upright
In their pebbled dish, all sweetness, winter-white.

Storm Season

Five pelicans in a wavering line
Hang on the wind
Rumpling the squall-colored sound.
Saltmarshes' silver mazes pock with rain.
This island's a curving fossil spine
In a broken white
Scree of breakers. Wet
Thunderheads pile like dirty rags above it.

Today no shrimper's nodding at its net.
Though the back taxes wait,
He steps outside for a smoke.
Another dead week—
In the kitchen his wife mutters at the sink.
Black weather gathers itself to break.

Detachment

These midlife nights, when I turn from you in bed,
It's not that I've stopped loving you. I've scented

Death, crouched nearby in its copse of shadows.
As the dying stop eating, drinking, speaking,

As they gather their rationed breaths for the plunge
Out of existence—no, wait, but that's not right.

The soul outlasts the knowledge of those who've said
Goodbye, returned to the clean white anteroom

Of the living with its nurses' stations, its flowers
That keep on blooming even when the name

On the card has emptied of its occupant.
The soul moves on. Likewise, the dying body,

Beginning to edge away by small degrees
From breath and thought, declines offers to sustain it.

Even now, against my better will my life,
Unschismed, girds itself for this departure:

No bag, no cloak, shaking the dust from its feet.
Tonight I'm falling asleep in my own arms,

Thinking that in that day when one of us
Awakes to find the sun still shining,

Other people still laughing and playing music,
Mail accruing in drifts on the kitchen table,

Clothes in the closet hanging unperturbed,
The dog, looking past the figure in the doorway,

Wagging his tail in confident expectation,
The last two beers waiting dewy in the fridge,

Then the hours will line up like empty glasses,
Too much for one person to drink alone

Without long practice, taken unawares.

White Morning, Crows

There are weddings every day,
All of them ours.

We marry the way the window
Clouds, by shapes

Breathed onto us, the dim spot
We write our names in,

Words that are clearest
When they evaporate.

We see through, not to what
We thought we meant

But to the irrelevant white lake,
The wind unfolding

Over the hill like a sheet
Shaken out on the line,

The crows. They speak a language
Distilled to one syllable,

Seamless and sharp
As what I want to say.

Their upright black strut
Stitches conversation

We can follow across the snow's
Mute face. One syllable:

The opacity it marks, stops,
Then marks again.

We see, then we don't. We say,
And we wait

For what we said to condense,
Come clear, be taken

Back into silence.
What can we promise

Except to breathe
In, breathe out?

To hear white space, air.
To hear how water

Takes the blank sky, becomes it,
How what happens when a crow

Stops for breath
Shapes the world.

Moonlight Sestina

The evening lengthens into dreamy sadness.
Across the street in soft blue rain a man is
Bending, windmilling, stretching his hamstrings, thinking
Himself unobserved. My brindle dog's on the watch,
However. Bristling, he glowers through the screen.
The man finishes stretching and moves off

Slowly, not quite running yet. Yes, off
You go, trudging stranger, lugging your sadness
Like ankle weights. Meanwhile, one mockingbird is
Tragedy enough. What is he thinking,
There on the fence, flipping his tail like a watch
Hand that points everywhere? On the screen

Porch the dog lies down. The fine-mesh screen,
Like a veil, keeps rain-light in, mosquitoes off.
It makes home movies of other people's sadness—
Real, imagined, hidden, whatever it is
They carry past my house at twilight. Thinking,
Deep in themselves, they don't notice that I watch

And wonder at them. Look, this girl with a sports watch
Stars in her own brief stop-action film. Then the screen
Goes blank. The uncredited extras have all stepped off-
Stage momentarily. Crape myrtles droop with a sadness
That's not human after all, but merely *is*,
A function of the universe's thinking.

I know what you're going to say: *What thinking?*
Perhaps the low-slung gray-green sky doesn't watch
Us after all. Perhaps it's only a screen
For the town's lights at night to bounce off,
Pink as cotton candy, no joy or sadness.
You might tell me, *Remember that the moon is*

Not a light—we only say it is
Because we like the word. Just now I'm thinking
I'd welcome moonlight's blue glow, like a watch
Face: *Look at the time!* Nose to the screen,
The dog moans in his throat. So much remains off-
Limits to him. Is the whole world made of sadness?

As the rain picks up, he and I watch through the screen.
Here again is the runner, all smiles, possibly thinking
He's peeled off, like a t-shirt, every sadness.

Lamplight

Having drawn the curtains, I stepped outside
And stood in the dark garden looking in—
Or not *in*, exactly. The curtains hid
Bookshelves, wardrobe, mirror, turned-back bed,
All the room's clear features. Still the linen

Leaked lamplight, a gold spill on the dry
Black stalks of black-eyed Susans beneath the window.
Behind its veil, the room shone privately
As with a happiness, a mystery to me.
I stood outside and wondered at that glow.

The night was huge around me, full of stars.
More light than theirs seemed hidden in that place,
Which looked at me, a masked, familiar face.
I looked back, night-veiled, strange, and out-of-doors.

My Father Drawing in an Upstairs Room

Outside, on a live stirring backdrop of broad-handed green,
The black cat on her branch spreads her back toes and licks, licks, between.

He looks musingly at her, and through her, as if right now he
Saw some mystery imposed on—or being born from—the tree.

On the table, five charcoal-drawn children roughhouse in a whiteness
You might see as *empty*. You might discern in it the likeness

Of a person who waits and observes, is as happy to wait
Forever for something to happen beyond these five straight

Black figures like capering trees in a cosmos of snow.
In my mind the catalpa leaves roofing the morning still glow,

Sun-heavy, alive. These five children he's caught in their white
Fleet-foot moment perdure, as all shadows survive on daylight.

He's looking at them, as in this long instant I've seen him.
Once more the cat spreads her black toes, once more licks between them.

For E.H., 1930–2005

Reunion

My grandfather stands on the front porch
Watching the dogs come back, reassembled

From hair, grit, eyeteeth. Again
The twin mares browse by the fence

In their brown-dust coats. Nobody asks
What they mean, appearing so suddenly.

In the back yard, the almost-forgotten
Dead—grandmothers in button shoes,

A first baby, never named—
Stay buried. It's not their overshoes

Lost in the grass behind the smokehouse.
Not their faces alive in anyone's

Memory. But my mother waits
In the pecan tree's fingered shadow:

A girl, still. A second daughter,
Straight hair braided tight.

Barefoot on the bare earth.
Holding a broken milk jug full

Of daylilies. Hesitating,
Needing someone to say, this once,

It's all right to be born now,
Now is as good a time as any.

Next month we'll find my grandfather's glasses
In their case beneath the front seat

Of his Oldsmobile. *Goodness*, my aunt will say,
As if it were a matter of his

Mislaying them. As if we all ought to
Want to give them back, as if

We'd missed our shot at absolution.
Suppose, though, the soul pauses

As it undoes its last buttons.
Looks back at us, framed in light

Behind the screen door. And we
Who are left step out into

This death, to be remembered.

Aunts

It was long ago, and they are dead.
I never knew them, but I think about them.
The story left untold becomes a story
I can tell myself until it's true.

I never knew them, but I think about them,
These grim ladies in black high-collared dresses.
I can tell myself until it's true
That they've been laughing. The camera turns on them,

And they are grim: three ladies, black high-collared dresses,
Three aunts posed beneath a catalpa tree.
They've been laughing. The camera turns on them
The weight of being seen forever like that—

Three aunts posed beneath a catalpa tree,
Unloved and unremembered, three brown names,
The weight of being seen forever. Like that,
They fade. The catalpa tree dissolves,

Unloved and unremembered, brown tree of names
No one can read, unraveling into the sky.
They fade, the catalpa tree dissolves,
A dark age overtakes them like sleep.

No one can read them. Unraveling into the sky
Like breath, their slender memory's unwritten.
A dark age overtakes them. While they sleep
I will tell their story to myself,

All breath, all the memories unwritten,
All the names wrong, the dates mis-guessed.
This is the story I keep telling myself—
What does time matter to a story?

So the names are wrong, the dates mis-guessed.
The sun's handprints among catalpa leaves
Are all the time that matters to this story
In which three women glower at a camera

Through sunlight handprinted by catalpa leaves,
A day on which anything might have happened
To these three who glower at the camera
Daring it to mistake them for the Fates.

On this day, anything might have happened.
All I know is that they stand there glowering.
Daring the camera. Looking like the Fates
Who stare down their own unknowable future.

I know that the three of them stand glowering.
They cannot imagine that I will see them
Stare down their own unknowable future,
Where I stand, on the far side of the grave.

Do they imagine someone like me? *Who will see us,*
They might be wondering. *Who will love us?*
Who will know us on the far side of the grave?
Does the long loneliness look back at them?

Well might they wonder, *Who will love us?*
The relatives they visited are dead.
The long loneliness has looked back at them,
And in that moment I don't know what they are doing,

Which relative, now dead, they are visiting,
Why they've gathered beneath the catalpa.
In that moment, what have they stopped doing?
Saved from time, what can they be thinking

While the white sun glares through the catalpa?
Though the story left untold becomes a story,
Time doesn't care what they were thinking.
They are dead, and it was long ago.

Laundromat

As in *laundromatic*, your washing done—
Done!—transfigured, made whiter, brighter,
By the alchemy of grainy vinyl floor,
Thin uremic light aging against
A windowful of sun, the sullen eyes
Of the woman whose bedroom slippers slap
Linoleum the way she'd like to slap
You, when you've let your clothes pool
Five seconds too long at the bottom
Of the dryer, your tumbled things steaming
Like the beagle you saw on the highway
Into town, laid open to the knife-
Edged morning air, the live heat escaping
Visibly through the torn skin, the soul
Climbing from its dog suit. Done.

Tracks

You follow those tracks up into the woods, you run into all kinds of wildlife. Moose, elk, you name it. You can get right up close to them.

        —*Hiker at the Blacks Fork River, Uinta Mountains, Utah*

But I don't want to follow them uphill,
Cleft prints that leave the river and climb
Through trees, until the trees give way

To a stone shelf that hides a hundred elk.
I don't want to turn up uninvited.
Last winter I watched an elephant

Travel across her cage, back up.
Fist-browed, she set her feet precisely
As if there were a map on the floor

To tell her how to walk through this life
Of finite distance, side to side,
To the small barred concrete horizon

And back. When the farm was sold,
My grandfather walked that way a while,
Staring among the tables and the lamps,

Seeing bird dogs rise from the rug,
A bean field unfold from the wall
Like a Murphy bed. I recognize that look:

The done deal, the decision, the eviction
Papers signed. Each morning the obituaries
Picture couple after couple, *Together Again*

After years of solitary dry-rot,
Of sleeping in the swaybacked bed alone,
Careful always not to cross that line—

Invisible, drawn at some point
When *sleeping together* began to mean *sleep*—
Between her side and his. The dead retreat

And don't exactly tell us not to follow.
They leave their shoes and spectacles for spoor.
Still, naked, barefoot, squinting, would they let us

Come close, call their names? Would they admit
To knowing us? The dry wind scouring
The ledges overhead is meant to scare us

Away from the high elevations,
The wild things that don't want finding,
The scree, sheer rock, enormous sky.

Commemorative Model

Glass and chrome, like a diner.
Like a Chrysler. Like the Chrysler building,
Its own personal skyline. In shelf-
Life vernacular, the KitchenAid blender
Can be said to *endure*. The yellow-lit
Night of my grandmother's kitchen
Endures too after its fashion: cat's
Fishy bowl beside the door, tall window
Above the sink filled with black darkness
Moving, speaking, pressing against the house
Which withstood it less and less.
One by one the old clocks stopped.
They remained on shelves as decoration.
You couldn't point out that it *wasn't*
3:47—you'd hurt their feelings.
Press any of the upright piano's
Ivories, yellowed as dentures,
And you'd hear a wet sponge of a note.
At the kitchen ceiling's ground-zero,
The bare bulb depending from its wire
Washed everything forty-watt clean:
Flecked linoleum peeling itself back
From the doorway like a letter steamed half-
Open, electric oven she poked with tongs
As if it were a fire, fearing the Tater Tots
Might at any time go up in flames.
You never know what might befall you
In the kitchen, all its minor conveniences

Conspiring not to warn you that sooner
Or later you'll confront obsolescence.
Eating time. Making everything sooner.
Microwaves, she muttered darkly. *Some such nonsense.*
She wouldn't have one. But inside
The Geneva cabinets' fuselage, her KitchenAid
Hunkered, furred with neglect.
Had she bought it? Did someone give it to her?
If you plugged it in, pressed a button, what
Would happen? Would it whip? grind? liquefy?
Explode? What price milkshakes, after all?
Or would its functions be reduced to one click,
A match not striking, the dull small
Voice of futility, like the Chrysler's
Pushbutton starter sparking nothing
For weeks after the wren's nest in the grille
Had emptied? She was someone, my grandmother,
Who possessed the dubious gift of charming
The inanimate world into silence
And disuse. In the end, she flew away
Clean, without grief, prepared
To beat egg whites into stiff peaks
Using nothing but a fork and her hand.

Dolphins

The winter harbor's rumple and fall,
Pewter-colored, slaps the pilings.
Black on a white sky, seagulls call,
     And pigeons walk the railings.
The day is full of wind and wings
And screams and wordless hungerings
Of a million seen and unseen things,
     And the salt grass grows.

From the pier's end you can see the tide
Reaching in and in and in.
Beneath its surge the dolphins ride.
     Now and then a fin
Rises, glossy-gray and thin,
A shadow on the water's skin—
You see it, then you don't again—
     And a wet breath blows.

They're driving in the schooling fish
Like bonfire-sparks a storm wind harries
Across a shifting, twilit grayish
     Sea-sky. From cold eyries
Of open wave, while daylight tarries
They stoop, strike, while the surge-tide carries
The flickering wide-eyed silver flurries
     Into dead-end shallows.

Intelligible, intelligent,
Undoubtingly at home in their
Breathless alien element,
      They share your human air.
Do they think like you? Can they possibly care
That you stand in the fitful sun up here,
While your eye searches and questions—*Where?*
      —and fellow-feeling follows?

As they rise from the gray cloudscape below,
Only their singular nostrils stare
Into this world where pelicans row
      Rough tides of wind. In the clear
Cold sun, their rolling bodies wear
The water's shine, as—there, and there—
They exhale, inhale, disappear,
      And the salt grass grows.

Bees

Consider how they comb the stiffening air
    In drag-leg flight. Here

      And there among the autumn blooms, a few
Persist: slower, somehow

Paler, too, as if their black-gold livery
    Bristled with early frost. There's a bravery

    In doing—
Whatever it is. Showing

The world, which may smile or may not notice,
    That you were born for this

      Work, this pilgrimage of habit. In brief light,
From skep to eyebright

And back again, the bees
    Perform as bees do everywhere, always:

    Fly, hover, fly
Some more, then—unpremeditated—die.

Grandmother Rising

She raised the window, heard the sycamore
Breathing darkness, cool invisible strands
Of air that seemed to lift her by her hands,
Stand her, turn her, loose her pinned-up hair,
Slip her through the screen. The blue wind bore
Her wingless body over fields and ponds
Till, skimming chimneys, clotheslines, raveled ends
Of cedar woods, she came to where the shore
Bared its one white shoulder. There, the moon
Drew a thumbnail-line as though to trace
A road where the sea pushed back the land.
Leaving her yellow nightgown on the sand,
Her image in the water's wrinkled face,
She waved like drying laundry and was gone.

Offering

The water was not so green then.
It had a roof for a sky. And people
Drowned curses in it, and wishes.
In the glass case, a brooch *of Irish
Make*: a golden circle, its ends
Bitten together by two lions' heads,
Its heavy pin made to pierce
A cloak's rough weave.

Someone's hands, steady or unsteady,
Worked it backward through the fabric.
Weighed it a moment, maybe,
Considering the price of homesickness,
Memory, dowry, bartering against
A goddess who boiled deeper than her waters.
Who might be induced to remember
One name. Forgot anyway.
Lost the petition, any record of an answer.
Cherished only what the asking cost.

Richeldis of Walsingham

In A.D. 1061, in Norfolk, not far from the North Sea coast, a Saxon widow named Richeldis de Faverches, Lady of the Manor of Walsingham, prayed for and received three visions. In these visions the Virgin Mary appeared to her and showed her the house at Nazareth where she had received the angel Gabriel's unexpected visit.

According to legend, the Virgin gave Richeldis the exact dimensions of this holy house and a directive to build a replica of it at Walsingham. This Richeldis did, though not without some trials. As the legend has it, she tried three times, unsuccessfully, to have the house built, according to what seem to have been unclear directions concerning its location. After a night of prayer she awoke to find that angels had built the house while she slept, on a site where a holy well was found to bubble from the ground.

Throughout the Middle Ages, Walsingham, called "England's Nazareth," remained a pilgrimage site, second only to Canterbury in its volume of pious traffic. Under Henry VIII, however, the king's own barefoot pilgrimages to Walsingham notwithstanding, the shrine was destroyed in 1538, its priests executed, and its devotion suppressed.

A Roman Catholic shrine, in the medieval Slipper Chapel, was restored in 1934. An Anglican shrine, featuring a rebuilt Holy House on the site of the miraculous spring, had opened in the 1920s.

biddan
  (to pray)

There is the rope's moan on the well-lip.
There is the cold sky, cloud-combed.
There is the sea, the headland's headdress,
Folding, folding, far afield,
Sun born from barn roofs, the tree-bare rise.
There is the lick of Lauds-bell, the wind's weeping.

Biddan: Ic bidde. We bidden.
Bed-making. Bidden, the soul's housewife sweeps
Clean the clod-cold hearth, furnishes fire
To see by, with sighs more wordful than words.

So she might have written.
So she surely said—*Ic bidde. We bidden.*
So I say, because her words lie hidden.

scryn
   (shrine)

Through green May softness every year, the people come
Barefoot into town, calling each other *Pilgrim*

In the self-conscious way that people do
When their world's ceased to believe. In a bow-

Window, forty various-sized Buddhas
Laugh at them—I wonder if they notice,

Or if the bust of Charles I above
The door opposite recalls them to what they love:

An England pocked with priest-holes, botched with blood.
Of course it was everyone's blood. It's always blood,

Blood and fire, burnt offering, the acceptable
Holocaust. Here, though, there waits no *hooly blissful*

Martir, only two or three bent cotton-haired
Ladies in cardigans, arm in arm. A whispered

Consultation, rooms, tea, and the public toilet,
Which might have been cleaner. Above the low houses, violet

Rainclouds bloom on the sky. In the pilgrims' hostel,
Where they've been vouchsafed a room, an American couple

Watch with mounting dismay as their two-year-old
Smears herself with red jelly and cream beneath the mild

Horrified gaze of more cardigan-armored ladies
Wearing nametags that say not *I am Church*, but *Gladys,*

Dilys, Sheila, strangers on a first-name basis,
Which perhaps, after all, is what the Church is—

Aliens sharing a glassy taste of holy water.
He Who Would Valiant Be. Candles that shudder

Across the Lady's gold impassive face.
A recurrent longing for something else.

richeldis

circa 1080

It's now—at this time of year—
I expect her. I sit in my low three-legged chair.

Spinning, spring firelight on the floor, pale weather.
Pear tree wreathed in dim blooms, the outer

Door propped as if at any moment someone
Might speak my name, or listen

As I sing to myself—*ic singe*—and watch this wool
Wind itself into something useful.

My hands that draw the twisted strands out long—
Blue-veined, knob-knuckled, stiffening.

My warm-flanked hounds
Sigh and twitch in the strewn rushes. All my grounds—

Little lambent curve of river, new-leafed trees
Catching at the wind as it hurries

In from the sea, hummocky meadow
Where one dun cow

Grazes her own shadow beneath the moon—
Swathed in time, this mortal earth sleeps alone.

stangefeall
  (fallen stones)

Stone door on the grass, portal from here to here.
Walk around. Walk through. Wherever you go, there you are,
In an avenue of gray stone, invisibly walled.
It's quiet there, and old.
In the bluebell woods, silence
Speaks in tongues. The eloquence
Of the small river moving always forward to the unseen
Sea is like the cherubim's, clean
With the cleanliness of humility, crying
Holy, hiding their eyes.

These things are made for dying:
Stone, and the hand that lays it on the earth.
These things are made for birth:
Wild iris swelling among their spears,
And in the well garden, years on years,
Frogspawn glittering stickily in algae,
Green and complicated as the rainy sky.

ham
(home)

1918

In waning light a clattering bus sets down
One traveler beside the village pump
Where the road forks, and the curve's quiet houses
Beneath their skeletal roses sit dark-eyed.
No lamps lit yet. It's only early
Afternoon, cold and gusty. She
Has to catch her hat before an updraft sends
It winging over the old priory wall.

That anything can stand: this still surprises her.
In her dreams she's always unrolling the endless bandages
Around endless ends of arms and legs, the faces
Chewed, spat out. Blood, and blood, and blood.
She can't wash her hands enough. *Like Lady Macbeth,*
She thinks wryly—*Funny I should feel that way,*
When it's not my fault. The fault is in our stars. . . .

She shakes herself and picks up her valise.
A town of women: that's what she's come home to.
Tomorrow Mother will have friends in to tea.
Nurse Cavell told me once—but no, she can't
Speak of things like that. It's over now.
Everything will be the way it was.

Mother's friends will say so over tea,
Even Mrs. Holm, whose John went walking
In the garden of the Somme—he was sown there.
Even Mrs. Carter, who lost two,
One at Verdun, one at Ypres. Her remaining
Stump, planted daily in the front window,
Speaks to no one. It's over now. Everything
Will be the way it was.

                              Well, there's a robin
Calling from the wall. A little flame
Of song in the cold, at home among
Gaunt archways and doors that lead to nowhere,
Stripped trees and the sharp green teeth of daffodils.
Everything will be the way it always is.
Swedes² with the Sunday roast. The vicar asked.
No curate, though. There are shortages of curates.
There are shortages, as well, of faith and hope.
And love. One cannot really hope for love.

---

2   turnips

duru
  (door)

Does an angel need a door?
Or is he simply *there*,
Where you thought
No one was? We're taught
To count our guardian
Angels, each a person
Occupying—not space,
Exactly; he's not a physical presence—
Perhaps it's enough to say
We count them.
                    He
More than counts. He wears
His name like a cloak of feathers:
Gabriel. Garment of fire.
Wind. A smell like fear
Or snow, that sharp blue
Outdoor scent. Who
Wouldn't startle, seeing
Him suddenly *being*
That thing we believe
In, made of knowing, and of love?

aefentid
  (eventide)

  1854

Corset strings must be left loose, then looser.
I'm sorry, ma'am. I can't pull harder than that.
Never mind, Ellis. I suppose we must resign ourselves.
The light's blue above the line of roofs.
Cold settles on the china jug and basin.
Soon he'll come walking up the road
From a burial—one of these people—
Prayer book in a pocket of his coat.

My hands fly over the bowl of winter jasmine.
Ellis cut it in the garden and brought it in.
My hands are white like moths. I'll go out in the spring.
There's a smell of mutton again. Will he say, *Mutton again*?

In London now the lamplighter will be going
Down the crescent touching all the posts with flame.
They'll be laughing by the fire in the drawing room.
Here there is only quiet and the smell of mutton.
Here a gray wall molders among bare trees.
Here there is only the road that divides at the pump
And runs away over the river and down to the sea.

þrines
  (trinity)

Here, their little daughter kneels in a pale dress
By a clump of bluebells, a small cool fire. In this

Image you see a trinity: child looked at,
Mother, father looking. One of them has got

The camera—that the other hovers near
Can't be presumed, only hoped for.

In those wet woods, the smell of rain, river, and stone
Is an atmosphere, complete. Let's say they move in it, all three,

Father, mother, child, the little trinity
Perfect in itself, but meant to grow

More life, as the stone's-throw ripples go
Widening over the river's fluid skin

And always to the sea are hastening down.

gemynd
  (memory)

1659

Our house is beautiful, very square
And golden. Its tall windows stare
Straight into the sun.
In the morning I walk in the garden.
Long ago it belonged to holy men—
I think they were holy, though
They were papists, and I am not to think so.
My brother and I look sometimes for
A holy well that's supposed to be here
And isn't. There is a well garden.
The well is full of frogs' eyes, golden
As the stone of our house. The stone
Arches in the garden stand sharply alone.
I feel sorry for them.
They seem
Like people I wish I had known.

richeldis

circa 1080

To sit companionably.
To say,

And how is it with you,
While the slow

Embers tick in the fireplace, the loom
Clacks and sighs, the room

Rests like a cat curled
On the wide windowsill of the world,

Looking out
Into the strangeness of the night

From its place
Of purring peace—

Another woman to riddle
Through the dark hours with, to sit in little

Wells of silence with, when speech
Falters, and each

Reads with sure, blind fingers the text
Of her own weaving, and doesn't mind what happens next.

brecan
  (to break)

  1538

In the night, we heard a sound of thunder.
Just now in the wet white morning light
My mother has come back from church—
Going for our water, was all she said, and
Mind you stay inside, Margery.
Keep the little ones inside, and out of the fire—

They are broken. Mother, Child, gone.
Faces shattered so that they aren't faces
But only bits of stone. My mother put them
Into her yoked buckets and brought them home.
Bits and pieces. *I didn't know what to do.*
They shouldn't lie there broken in the rain.

Now they lie broken on our table.
An eye, a smile. All the saints are headless,
My mother says. Her voice is tight and dry.
When I ask where my father is today,
And what they will have done with Father Walter,
And how we all will hear the Mass without him,
She shrugs and turns again to mend the fire.
The turnips roast like heads among the coals.

fisc
  (fish)

Beneath the bank's overhang
Fingerlings hide:
Silver streaks, glancing
Sunlight on a road
With trees overhead,
Woven and wavering,
Touched by wind
Like a current meandering
Back, undecided,
To its spawning
Bed.

In the church they are saying
Mass. Outside,
The world is praying.
Without a word,
The sun's tracing
Trout-shapes on mud.

halig dag
(holiday)

1401

I'm run off my feet.
No: my feet are still there.
All night the blood pounds inside them.
Ale, ale. Fleas in the bed?
Well, of course there are fleas.
My own bed has fleas.
Fleas never hurt a body. Ale, ale.
You would think a drink of holy water,
Bubbling cold from the entrails of the world,
Out of mystery, tasting like metal—
If you could drink a new blade—tasting
Like the earth's true cold thin blood
Given for you—you would think, after that,
That nobody would ever cry for ale
Without at least a good tale to trade for it.

Hidden behind the wall, a bell is calling.
All very well for the canons. Up at three
To pray? I'm up at three to put the new bread in
And chase the last ropy cockerel round the yard.
This soup's more holy water than cabbage,
Said a man only yesterday. There's chicken
In it, too, I told him, straight. Every day
Save Friday. Then it's fish seethed in milk.
Mistress? Mistress?—God save you,
No more beds here. Go along

To the Slipper Chapel. Say your prayers, pilgrim.
God found Our Lord a bed. Ale, ale.
Let Him—God save us—find you,
By Our Lady, a clean straw bed without fleas.

wendan
  (to turn)

The Fakenham bus stops beside the pump.
There is one bus for Fakenham on Saturdays.
There are no rooms left to let in the town.
It is the pilgrimage. You understand
And so will flee for Norwich and the train.
London will receive you into its
Surprisingly quiet bosom, after all this:
Tall house in the Crescent, German friends
Laying the long table with *broetchen* and cheese,
Rooms filled with the brown smell of coffee
And secular calm. There nobody argues over
Comparative qualities of incense, or whether
In an icon Our Lady may appear with the Apostle John—
Her immediate family ONLY, says a man,
Thumping the tea-shop table with clenched fist.

There is the one bus for Fakenham on Saturdays.
It stops beside the pump, and so,
There where the village road's cleft—a forked stick,
Dowsing the way back into the world—
You are waiting with your luggage and your child,
All piled at the foot of the pump like offerings
Retched up from the dark corners of tents
And brought to Aaron to be melted down
While Moses loiters on the cloven mountain—
Silly American family, who forget
Which side of the English road is which,
Silly Americans who have not realized
That the four corners of Norfolk contain the world.

There is the one bus for Fakenham on Saturdays.
When we say, *Stops at the pump*, of course we mean it
Metaphorically. What's literal is that this
Is the weekend for the pilgrimage, and already
People are pouring barefoot into the town
Past the pump, past you, and into the rooms
Where no longer is there any room for you,
And the bus, which stops at the pub across from the pump,
The one Saturday bus, has already gone
Roaring across the sandy hills for Fakenham.

wif
(*woman*)

1349

Thirty to my fourteen: my wedded lord.
The church so cold our white breaths colored

The air, small clouds
The shape of words
I scarcely remembered afterwards.

I was handed onto the horse,
Which shied beneath me. Its rough rackety pace

Bore me east. The hilly road unrolled
Across a mounded field.
Behind me, the long bell tolled.

I practiced marriage. Learned. Then sickness took
Him. The joiner and the cook

Died, too.
I sat beside him through

One watery day, then a night so clear
I could hear

A cock crow across a distant field.
His hand cooled in mine. His face stilled

Into something so unlike itself that I
Already couldn't see

Gray light behind his eyes, the flush
Wind raised in his cheeks. *Flesh of my flesh,*

He called me. *Bone of my bone.*
Now he's stone.

Each morning at Mass
My shadow falls across
His staring face

Graven into the floor. Once
I went back alone and knelt to kiss
The polished slab that keeps his bones in place.

modor
  (mother)

  1216

In dreams I find my Geoffrey up the sycamore.
At his going, all the yellow tree-hands clamor.

I can see you down there,
Mother. You're eating up my pear.

My teeth cringe at the grainy-sweet
Fruit-flesh, and at his shout

As he falls from the swagged sky
With a crack and a thud. *Breathe, Mother. Did I die?*

Today he's written to me from Brindisi, black thick-jointed words
That fly across the vellum page like blackbirds

Crying their one foreign syllable,
Perfectly intelligible

To themselves. Shading my eyes with one hand,
I watch them as they bank against the wind

And send their delegations down to roost,
One choir at a time, in the tallest

Yew tree. Sunsets, I hear them
Yammering as the sky drops its hem

Over the red underskirts of day
And wonder what it is they have to say.

sceadu
  (shadow)

A lost doorway holds a slanted shadow
That looks on a demolished island, fallow

Still in a rare whitewash of moonlight.
Could it live there, with no sun to cast it

But memory, through the quiet rains
These dank spring mornings, across the ordered ruins

Of an older, more disintegrated world
Sinking daily into the wet unplanted field?

Shall the shades rise now and praise?
Does the soul, when it leaves the body's house

And turns the blind corner, sing as it goes?
Does it whistle? Who will listen for the shadows

In their valleys, in their alleyways, at their doors,
As they lean from their mystery into ours?

brimfugol
(seabird)

1101

In the morning I hear them crying
As if they had lost their way.
I have never seen the sea.
This bright morning my mistress is dying

And taking her time about it. I have come
From the dim house into the springing green
Of the well garden, to skim
Green scum and frogspawn from the otherwise clean

Well-water—not the holy well.
Yesterday Father Gervais anointed her.
She could not swallow. I think the very ill
Know that soon they will be offered more

Than they can hold, that Christ Himself will feed
Them from His own torn breast.
Christ the bird will tear Himself and bleed,
And truly they at last will feast.

The housefolk here don't like it when I loiter
Too long here with the sky-high voices
Crying *L'eau, l'eau,* above the homely *waeter.*
All the while this earth—green, heedless—rejoices.

richeldis
  circa 1080

My soul's great with remembering. In my room
I kneel to pray beside the woven pilgrim

Whose flat road stops just short of the raveled
Hem. How odd the untraveled

Air of this world, my own,
Must look to him, all staff and shell and frown.

Stitches fall like footprints across snow
In murky rushlight. Now—

The little flame shivers in the wind.
The curtain's sudden flutter might be a hand

Waving smoke away. Some wing
Treads the dark air, whispering.

My needle's poised, a dragonfly. The window
Stands open to the night. An unfurled shadow

—Owl?—drifts across the moonlit grass.
It seems to me the hand of God could pass

Over this house again and spill
What it will, its weightless seed swell.

hus
  (house)

High heaven harrowed a dew-fallow field,
Planted what pleased it. The first building blundered:
Square, Saxon-style. Wrong.
Bad in its bones, the treasure-ship sank.
Each day the doing mocked and unmade me.

Dawn-draft on the dry grass.
The world washed, gray, bending
To summon a singing, a song-rush descending
Of something like wings. A wind-rowing soul
Escaping or coming. A sky-going angel
Sailing the cloud-sea from high heaven's hall,
Door open, then shut again. And is that all?
Through day-dusk, a dim shape
In mist: memory, hope.
But where is she who would keep the house here?
Rope moans on the well-lip. The tree stands bare.

My unmaking made this.

SALLY THOMAS was born in Memphis, Tennessee, in 1964, and was educated at Vanderbilt University, the University of Memphis, and the University of Utah. She spent some years living in the American West and in Great Britain before settling in North Carolina, her current home. She is the author of two poetry chapbooks, *Fallen Water* (2015) and *Richeldis of Walsingham* (2016), both from Finishing Line Press. Over the last two decades, her poetry and fiction have appeared in *Dappled Things, First Things, Relief: A Journal of Art and Faith, Southern Poetry Review*, the *New Yorker*, the *Rialto*, and other journals in the United States and Great Britain.

ALSO FROM ABLE MUSE PRESS

Jacob M. Appel, *The Cynic in Extremis – Poems*

William Baer, *Times Square and Other Stories;*
New Jersey Noir – A Novel;
New Jersey Noir: Cape May – A Novel

Lee Harlin Bahan, *A Year of Mourning (Petrarch) – Translation*

Melissa Balmain, *Walking in on People (Able Muse Book Award for Poetry)*

Ben Berman, *Strange Borderlands – Poems;*
Figuring in the Figure – Poems

Lorna Knowles Blake, *Green Hill (Able Muse Book Award for Poetry)*

Michael Cantor, *Life in the Second Circle – Poems*

Catherine Chandler, *Lines of Flight – Poems*

William Conelly, *Uncontested Grounds – Poems*

Maryann Corbett, *Credo for the Checkout Line in Winter – Poems;*
Street View – Poems
In Code – Poems

John Philip Drury, *Sea Level Rising – Poems*

Rhina P. Espaillat, *And after All – Poems*

Anna M. Evans, *Under Dark Waters: Surviving the* Titanic *– Poems*

D. R. Goodman, *Greed: A Confession – Poems*

Margaret Ann Griffiths, *Grasshopper – The Poetry of M A Griffiths*

Katie Hartsock, *Bed of Impatiens – Poems*

Elise Hempel, *Second Rain – Poems*

Jan D. Hodge, *Taking Shape – carmina figurata;*
The Bard & Scheherazade Keep Company – Poems

Ellen Kaufman, *House Music – Poems*

Emily Leithauser, *The Borrowed World (Able Muse Book Award for Poetry)*

Hailey Leithauser, *Saint Worm – Poems*

Carol Light, *Heaven from Steam – Poems*

Kate Light, *Character Shoes – Poems*

April Lindner, *This Bed Our Bodies Shaped – Poems*

Martin McGovern, *Bad Fame – Poems*

Jeredith Merrin, *Cup* – *Poems*

Richard Moore, *Selected Poems;*
   The Rule That Liberates: An Expanded Edition – *Selected Essays*

Richard Newman, *All the Wasted Beauty of the World* – *Poems*

Alfred Nicol, *Animal Psalms* – *Poems*

Deirdre O'Connor, *The Cupped Field* *(Able Muse Book Award for Poetry)*

Frank Osen, *Virtue, Big as Sin* *(Able Muse Book Award for Poetry)*

Alexander Pepple (Editor), *Able Muse Anthology;*
   Able Muse – *a review of poetry, prose & art* (issues from winter 2010 on)

James Pollock, *Sailing to Babylon* – *Poems*

Aaron Poochigian, *The Cosmic Purr* – *Poems;*
   Manhattanite *(Able Muse Book Award for Poetry)*

Tatiana Forero Puerta, *Cleaning the Ghost Room* – *Poems*

Jennifer Reeser, *Indigenous* – *Poems*

John Ridland, *Sir Gawain and the Green Knight (Anonymous)* – *Translation;*
   Pearl (Anonymous) – *Translation*

Stephen Scaer, *Pumpkin Chucking* – *Poems*

Hollis Seamon, *Corporeality* – *Stories*

Ed Shacklee, *The Blind Loon: A Bestiary*

Carrie Shipers, *Cause for Concern* *(Able Muse Book Award for Poetry)*

Matthew Buckley Smith, *Dirge for an Imaginary World* *(Able Muse Book Award for Poetry)*

Susan de Sola, *Frozen Charlotte* – *Poems*

Barbara Ellen Sorensen, *Compositions of the Dead Playing Flutes* – *Poems*

Rebecca Starks, *Time Is Always Now* – *Poems*

Rosemerry Wahtola Trommer, *Naked for Tea* – *Poems*

Wendy Videlock, *Slingshots and Love Plums* – *Poems;*
   The Dark Gnu and Other Poems;
   Nevertheless – *Poems*

Richard Wakefield, *A Vertical Mile* – *Poems*

Gail White, *Asperity Street* – *Poems*

Chelsea Woodard, *Vellum* – *Poems*

www.ablemusepress.com

CPSIA information can be obtained
at www.ICGtesting.com
Printed in the USA
LVHW091118090620
657724LV00007B/1265

9 781773 490434